Horseradish

BITTER TRUTHS YOU CAN'T AVOID

EGMONT PRESS: ETHICAL PUBLISHING

Egmont Press is about turning writers into successful authors and children into passionate readers – producing books that enrich and entertain. As a responsible children's publisher, we go even further, considering the world in which our consumers are growing up.

Safety First
Naturally, all of our books meet legal safety requirements. But we go further than this; every book with play value is tested to the highest standards – if it fails, it's back to the drawing-board.

Made Fairly
We are working to ensure that the workers involved in our supply chain – the people that make our books – are treated with fairness and respect.

Responsible Forestry
We are committed to ensuring all our papers come from environmentally and socially responsible forest sources.

For more information, please visit our website at
www.egmont.co.uk/ethicalpublishing

Lemony Snicket

Horseradish

BITTER TRUTHS
YOU CAN'T AVOID

EGMONT

EGMONT

We bring stories to life

First published in Great Britain 2007
by Egmont UK Limited
239 Kensington High Street
London W8 6SA
First published in the USA 2007
by HarperCollins Children's Books

Published by arrangement
with HarperCollins Children's Books
a division of HarperCollins Publishers, Inc.
1350 Avenue of the Americas, New York,
New York 10019, USA

Text copyright © 2007 Lemony Snicket
Photographs copyright © 2007 Mark Tucker/Merge Left Reps., Inc.

Typography by Alison Donalty

ISBN 978 1 4052 3413 9

1 3 5 7 9 10 8 6 4 2

A CIP catalogue record for this title is available from the British Library

Printed and bound in Great Britain by the CPI Group

Horseradish

BITTER TRUTHS YOU CAN'T AVOID

INTRODUCTION

There is an old story which may or may not
interest you but nevertheless will be the bulk
of this introduction, the way a horrid breakfast
can be the bulk of your morning or a long car
chase can be the bulk of your week. The story
concerns a woman who lived in a small grass
hut with her husband, in a remote village
surrounded by an enormous field of horseradish, which is a very bitter root. Like many
people, the woman and her husband did not
care for horseradish, so every morning the
woman would fish for lake snails, while her
husband would gather raisins in the fields,

and each night they would have a horrid meal of raisin-stuffed snails. After several years of this, the woman began to wonder something.

"Husband," she wondered out loud one evening, "life must be more than sitting at home doing the same thing over and over, don't you think?"

"Beats me," said her husband, with his mouth full of snail. "But the other day your mother was telling me about a wise man who lives on top of a mountain someplace. He'd probably know."

"That's interesting," the woman said, and excused herself from the table to walk to the next-door hut, where her mother was sitting on a grass sofa, gazing out a grass window at the field of horseradish and cutting her toenails. "What's this I hear about a wise man?" the woman asked her mother, wondering if life was more than watching one's relatives do unpleasant things.

"Miss Matmos told me about him," the

woman's mother said, struggling with a particularly difficult toenail.

"Miss Matmos?" the woman repeated.
"You mean my old third-grade teacher?"

"She lives on the other side of the horseradish field, near the fishing pole storage
facility," the woman's mother said, "and she
was saying something about a wise old man
who lives on the top of a mountain."

The woman hurried through the field of
horseradish to the fishing pole storage facility,
where every day she hung her fishing pole next
to all the other fishing poles for safekeeping.
Sure enough, Miss Matmos was sitting nearby,
writing insults in the margins of her students'
papers. The woman watched her old third-
grade teacher scrawl "You're an idiot!" in bright
red ink, and wondered if life was more than the
grim tasks one must perform at school and at
work. "Miss Matmos," she asked, "I was wondering if you knew anything about a wise man
who lives on the top of a mountain."

"Well," said Miss Matmos, "the mountain is very far away, and the climb is very difficult and quite dull. If you're going to go, I'd suggest you take a book with you."

Miss Matmos handed the woman a book and sent her on her way, which was as far, difficult, and dull as the third-grade teacher had described it. As the woman walked the hundreds of miles to the mountain, she read the book to tatters, and although it was a wonderful story called *A High Wind in Jamaica,* she could not help wondering if life was more than being entertained by literature. As she made her way through the thorny bushes that grew at the base of the mountain, she grew exhausted and thought sadly of her husband, and she wondered if life was more than traveling from one place to another, suffering from poor emotional health and pondering the people one loves. As she climbed the mountain's monotonous peaks, she stared down at some people at the bottom of the mountain, who appeared to be doing something suspicious, and stared up at the dull gray flowers that grew in the mountain's cracks, and she wondered about people who lead a life of mystery, and about the mysteries of life. As she approached the top of the mountain, where she could see the condominium owned by the wise man, it grew very dark, and the woman wondered about the overall feeling of doom that one cannot ever escape no matter what one does. She grew closer and closer, and kept wondering about all the things she had been wondering about for all these many months, as well as miscellaneous things that I have neglected to mention in specific. Finally, the woman was so high up that her grass hut was merely a faraway green speck, and the horseradish field a tiny, bitter square, but without even a glance at where she had come from, she knocked on the door of the condominium, and within moments she was facing the man she had come all this way to see.

"O, great wise man," she said, "I have been wondering so many things. Is life more than sitting at home doing the same thing over and over? Wise man, is life more than watching one's relatives do unpleasant things, or more than the grim tasks one must perform at school and at work? Is life more than being entertained by literature, wise man, or more than traveling from one place to another, suffering from poor emotional health and pondering the people one loves? And what about those who lead a life of mystery? And the mysteries of life? And, wise man, what about the overall feeling of doom that one cannot ever escape no matter what one does, and miscellaneous things that I have neglected to mention in specific?"

But the man was already shaking his head. "You have it all wrong," he said. "I'm not a wise man—I'm a *wide* man."

He took a step closer to her, and sure

enough the woman could see that he was substantially overweight, particularly around the hips. "Then you don't know the answers to my questions?" she asked.

"No," the man said. "And furthermore, this is private property."

With a slam of the door and a rude "Harrumph," the man was gone, and the woman began her long, difficult, and dull journey all the way back to her home. When she finally approached the grass huts, quite tired and extremely hungry, she saw her mother sitting on the front grass stoop, cleaning her ears with a long, slender pole the woman recognized at once.

"That's my fishing pole!" said the woman. "I need it for work!"

"Where in the world have you been?" the woman's mother asked. "You walked away in the middle of our conversation! I didn't hear from you for months, so I assumed you didn't want your fishing pole anymore."

"I've been on a long, disappointing journey," the woman replied. "Aren't you even going to welcome your daughter home?"

"I have a new daughter," the mother bragged, and then called into her hut. "Come on out, sweetie!"

To the woman's surprise, Miss Matmos stepped out of the hut, dressed in a long, white bridal gown. Following alongside was the woman's husband, who was wearing a tuxedo.

"You just got up in the middle of dinner and left for many months," explained the husband, "so now I'm getting myself a new wife, who asks fewer questions than you do."

"I'd invite you to the wedding feast," said the woman's mother, "but I don't want to. Now please excuse us—the wedding procession is about to begin."

The woman heard a fanfare of kazoos, and saw that many of her neighbors had gathered to usher the bridal couple to the far corner of the horseradish field, where a rabbi was waiting to marry them. The woman's mother led the way, followed by the husband and Miss Matmos, and before long the woman was all alone, still quite tired and extremely hungry. Knowing that she would not get a bite of the catered food at the wedding feast, she tugged a horseradish root out of the ground and gnawed at it glumly. As the bitter taste invaded the woman's mouth— the same mouth that had asked all those questions to which she still did not know the answers—the new bride turned around and called out one last thing to her.

"By the way," said Miss Matmos, "I was going over my old grade books, and it turns out you flunked third grade."

The moral of this story, if you are interested, is that there are bitter truths you cannot avoid in this world, whether you are wondering about home, family, school, work, entertainment, literature, travel, emotional health, affairs of the heart, a life of mystery, the mystery of life, an overall feeling of doom that one cannot ever escape no matter what one does, and miscellaneous things that I have neglected to mention in specific. For your convenience, some of these bitter truths have been placed into this somewhat handy book, and arranged into thirteen chapters so that any time you are wondering about something, you can open the book and read a bitter truth or two, rather than go to the trouble of trying to find a wise man, particularly in your neighborhood where so few of them live.

I

HOME

The difference between
a house and a home is like
the difference between
a man and a woman—
it might be embarrassing
to explain,
but it would be very
unusual to get
them confused.

There is something
marvelous about returning
home at the end of
a long day, even if there
is tuna fish for dinner.

There are some people
who believe that home is
where one hangs one's hat,
but these people tend to
live in closets and
on little pegs.

An old cowboy song
celebrates home on the range,
where deer and antelope play,
but anyone who has seen deer
and antelope knows that
when they are frolicking
they scarcely look where
they are flinging their hooves,
which is why cowboys have
been pummeled almost
to extinction.

It is always sad when
someone leaves home,
unless they are simply going
around the corner and will return
in a few minutes with
ice-cream sandwiches.

One's home is like a delicious piece of pie you order in a restaurant on a country road one cozy evening—the best piece of pie you have ever eaten in your life—and can never find again. After you leave home, you may find yourself feeling homesick, even if you have a new home that has nicer wallpaper and a more efficient dishwasher than the home in which you grew up, and no matter how many times you visit you may never quite cure yourself of the fluttery, homesick feeling in your stomach. Homesickness can even strike you when you are still living at home, but a home that has changed over the years, and you long for the time—even if such a time existed only in your imagination—when your home was as delicious as you remember. You may search your family and your mind—just as you might search dark and winding country roads—trying to recapture the best time in your life, so that you might cure your homesickness with a second slice of that distant, faraway pie, but your search will end in vain, as you have lost the map that told you where to turn, and the restaurant has long ago burned down, and the baker who made the pie has gotten tired of waiting for you and has devoted her life to making tomato paste instead, but she is no good at it, and now you are lost in life, the darkness closing in on you, with nothing but a sad flutter in your stomach and a sour acidic taste in your mouth.

An American writer of
my acquaintance titled one
of his books
You Can't Go Home Again,
but he was not necessarily
talking to you.

2

FAMILY

Perhaps if we saw what
was ahead of us,
and glimpsed the crimes,
follies, and misfortunes
that would befall us later on,
we would all stay in our
mother's wombs, and then
there would be nobody in the
world but a great number of
very fat, very irritated women.

A certain Russian writer said that happy families are all alike, which is absurd. Some happy families do nothing but train seals all day, while others prefer to paint pictures of flowers on pieces of pottery and sell them for outrageous prices at fairs. There are happy families who consist of nothing but a happy father and his happy twin sons, and there are happy families who have so many happy cousins that whenever the happy family wants to go somewhere together they have to rent an entire happy bus to do so. There are happy families who live in the happy center of certain happy cities, and there are happy families who rent a different happy hut on a different happy island every happy week. Really the only thing that all happy families have in common is happiness and perhaps a certain sagginess around the cheeks from smiling all the livelong day.

Unless you are a hermit or half of a pair of Siamese twins, you probably enjoy taking the occasional break from members of your family to enjoy some privacy, perhaps with a friend or companion, in your room or in a railway car you have managed to sneak aboard.

There are some who say that you should forgive everyone, even the people who have disappointed you immeasurably. There are others who say you should not forgive anyone, and should stomp off in a huff no matter how many times they apologize. Of these two philosophies, the second one is of course much more fun, but it can also grow exhausting to stomp off in a huff every time someone has disappointed you, as everyone disappoints everyone eventually, and one can't stomp off in a huff every minute of the day.

Siblings who claim to get along
all the time are most
definitely hiding something.

Arguing with somebody

is never pleasant,

but sometimes it is useful

and necessary to do so.

Babies pop into this world in the usual way, and from that moment the babies' families have to do their best to guess what might make the baby happy, like guessing the answer to a riddle. But many riddles are difficult to guess, which is why one sees so many babies crying their little eyes out, as if they wished they could simply pop back out of the world the way they came.

Temper tantrums, however
fun they may be to throw,
rarely solve whatever problem
is causing them.

It is not very polite to interrupt a person, of course, but sometimes if the person is very unpleasant you can hardly stop yourself.

One day, when your mother is yelling at you, you might begin to hear a tiny voice in your head that will tell you that you are right and your mother is wrong. Over the years, this voice might get louder and louder, and you might find that you prefer listening to this voice instead of your mother's voice, particularly if she has been yelling at you this whole time.

3
SCHOOL

A long time ago, there was
no such thing as school,
and children spent their days
learning a trade, a phrase which
here means "standing around
doing tedious tasks under the
instruction of a bossy adult."
In time, however, people
realized that the children
could be allowed to sit, and
the first school was invented.

The expression
"Those who can't do, teach"
is a curious one,
because if you look at the
world, you'll see that teachers
aren't particularly worse at
doing things than anyone else,
so perhaps the expression
might be better worded as
"Nobody can do anything."

Most schools have a system of loud bells, which startle the students and teachers at regular intervals and remind them that time is passing even more slowly than it seems.

Anyone who asks you to describe your summer vacation in writing probably has a secret, infernal plan, and under no circumstances should you include in your report even a hint of the truth.

Recess is a part of the
school day designed to give
children a break from the
more unpleasant aspects of
the educational system,
but so many school yards are
full of villainous students
that recess can often turn
out to be the most
unpleasant part of the day.

If you try to avoid every instance of peer pressure you will end up without any peers whatsoever, and the trick is to succumb to enough pressure that you do not drive your peers away, but not so much that you end up in a situation in which you are dead or otherwise uncomfortable. This is a difficult trick, and most people never master it, and end up dead or uncomfortable at least once during their lives.

Oftentimes, when people
are miserable, they will
want to make other
people miserable, too.
But it never helps.

4
WORK

In most cases,
the best strategy for a
job interview is to be
fairly honest, because the
worst thing that can happen
is that you won't get the job
and will spend the rest of your
life foraging for food in the
wilderness and seeking shelter
underneath a tree or the
awning of a bowling alley that
has gone out of business.

Business cards, of course, are not proof of anything. Anyone can go to a print shop and have cards made that say anything they like. The king of Denmark can order business cards that say he sells golf balls. Your dentist can order business cards that say she is your grandmother. In order to escape from the castle of an enemy of mine, I once had cards printed that said I was an admiral in the French navy. Just because something is typed—whether it is typed on a business card or typed in a newspaper or book—this does not mean that it is true.

Fetching objects for people
who are too lazy to fetch
them for themselves is never
a pleasant task, particularly
when the people
are insulting you.

A newspaper, as I'm sure you know, is a collection of supposedly true stories written down by writers who either saw them happen or talked to people who did. These writers are called journalists, and like telephone operators, butchers, ballerinas, and people who clean up after horses, journalists can sometimes make mistakes.

It has been said that the
hardest job in the world is
raising a child, but the people
who say this have probably
never worked at a comb
factory or captured pirates
on the high seas.

Just because something is
traditional is no reason
to do it, of course.
Piracy, for example,
is a tradition that has been
carried on for hundreds of
years, but that doesn't mean
we should all attack ships
and steal their gold.

Members of your family might say they are working hard all day long, while you are off at school or clarinet lessons, but the only way to know this for sure is to follow them at a discreet distance.

Labor Day is a holiday honoring those who work for a living. Laborious Day is a lesser known holiday honoring those who cannot stop talking about their work.

Like people, animals will
become frightened and likely
do whatever you say if you
whip them enough.

5
ENTERTAINMENT

It is one of life's bitterest truths that bedtime so often arrives just when things are really getting interesting.

People often suggest, when there is no enter-tainment available, that one twiddle one's thumbs. Twiddling one's thumbs simply refers to an activity in which one's thumbs are rotated quickly in tiny, continuous circles, and twiddling one's thumbs is even more tiresome than the people who suggest twid-dling one's thumbs think, so I recommend that the next time someone suggests you twiddle your thumbs you find something else to twiddle instead.

When people ask you if you play
a certain sport, it is likely that
they are very good at that sport
and are hoping you are only
mediocre so that you can waste
an afternoon losing a game.
In such instances the safest action
is to run away very quickly as
soon as the question is asked.

An apocryphal story—the word "apocryphal" here means "obviously untrue"—tells of two people, long ago, who were very bored, and that instead of complaining about it they sat up all night and invented the game of chess so that everyone else in the world, on evenings when there is nothing to do, can also be bored by the perplexing and tedious game they invented.

One of the world's most
popular entertainments is a
deck of cards, which contains
thirteen each of four suits,
highlighted by kings, queens,
and jacks, who are possibly
the queen's younger,
more attractive boyfriends.

Wishing, like sipping a glass of punch, or pulling aside a bearskin rug in order to access a hidden trapdoor in the floor, is merely a quiet way to spend one's time before the candles are extinguished on one's birthday cake.

Entertaining a notion, like entertaining a baby cousin or entertaining a pack of hyenas, is a dangerous thing to refuse to do. If you refuse to entertain a baby cousin, the baby cousin may get bored and entertain itself by wandering off and falling down a well. If you refuse to entertain a pack of hyenas, they may become restless and entertain themselves by devouring you. But if you refuse to entertain a notion—which is just a fancy way of saying that you refuse to think about a certain idea—you have to be much braver than someone who is merely facing some bloodthirsty animals, or some parents who are upset to find their little darling at the bottom of a well, because nobody knows what an idea will do when it goes off to entertain itself.

There is one, and only one, advantage to somebody who cannot play the violin insisting on doing so anyway, and the advantage is that they often play so loudly that they cannot hear if the audience is having a conversation.

A good thing to do when

one is sitting, eating,

and resting is to

have a conversation.

It is always cruel to laugh at people, of course, although sometimes if they are wearing an ugly hat it is hard to control yourself.

One of the world's tiresome questions is what object one would bring to a desert island, because people always answer "a deck of cards" or "*Anna Karenina*" when the obvious answer is "a well-equipped boat and a crew to sail me off the island and back home where I can play all the card games and read all the Russian novels I want."

Everyone should be able to do
one card trick, tell two jokes,
and recite three poems,
in case they are ever trapped
in an elevator.

6
LITERATURE

No matter who you are,

no matter where you live,

and no matter how many

people are chasing you,

what you don't read is

often as important as

what you do read.

An associate of mine once wrote a novel called *Corridors of Power*, which told the story of various people discussing how the world has become a corrupt and dangerous place and whether or not there are enough people with the integrity and decency necessary to keep the entire planet from descending into despair. I have not read this novel in several years, because I participate in enough discussions on how the world has become a corrupt and dangerous place and whether or not there are enough people with the integrity and decency necessary to keep the entire planet from descending into despair without reading about it in my leisure time.

It is much, much worse to receive bad news through the written word than by somebody simply telling you, and I'm sure you understand why. When somebody simply tells you bad news, you hear it once, and that's the end of it. But when bad news is written down, whether in a letter or a newspaper or on your arm in felt tip pen, each time you read it, you feel as if you are receiving the news again and again.

There are those who say
that life is like a book,
with chapters for each event
in your life and a limited
number of pages on which
you can spend your time.
But I prefer to think that
a book is like a life,
particularly a good one,
which is well worth staying
up all night to finish.

A good library will never be

too neat, or too dusty,

because somebody will

always be in it,

taking books off the shelves

and staying up late

reading them.

A library is like an island in
the middle of a vast sea
of ignorance, particularly
if the library is very tall
and the surrounding
area has been flooded.

If writers wrote as carelessly
as some people talk, then
adhasdh asdglaseuyt[bn[
pasdlgkhasdfasdf.

Sometimes

words

are

not

enough.

7
TRAVEL

There are times to stay put,

and what you want will come

to you, and there are times to

go out into the world and find

such a thing for yourself.

What happens in a certain
place can stain your feelings
for that location,
just as ink can stain a
white sheet.
You can wash it, and wash it,
and still never forget
what has transpired,
a word which here means
"happened and made
everybody sad."

A passport, as I'm sure you

know, is a document that one

shows to government officials

whenever one reaches a

border between countries,

so the officials can

learn who you are,

where you were born,

and how you look when

photographed unflatteringly.

Deciding whether or not to
trust a person is like deciding
whether or not to climb a tree,
because you might get a wonderful
view from the highest branch,
or you might simply get covered
in sap, and for this reason many
people choose to spend their
time alone and indoors,
where it is harder to
get a splinter.

There are some who say that sitting at home reading is the equivalent of travel, because the experiences described in the book are more or less the same as the experiences one might have on a voyage, and there are those who say that there is no subsitute for venturing out into the world. My own opinion is that it is best to travel extensively but to read the entire time, hardly glancing up to look out of the window of the airplane, train, or hired camel.

When you are traveling by bus, it is always difficult to decide whether you should sit in a seat by the window, a seat on the aisle, or a seat in the middle. If you take an aisle seat, you have the advantage of being able to stretch your legs whenever you like, but you have the disadvantage of people walking by you, and they can accidentally step on your toes or spill something on your clothing. If you take a window seat, you have the advantage of getting a clear view of the scenery, but you have the disadvantage of watching insects die as they hit the glass. If you take a middle seat, you have neither of these advantages, and you have the added disadvantage of people leaning all over you when they fall asleep. You can see at once why you should always arrange to hire a limousine or rent a mule rather than take the bus to your destination.

Never trust anyone

who has not brought

a book with them.

8

EMOTIONAL
HEALTH

I'm sure you have heard it said that appearance does not matter so much, and that it is what's on the inside that counts. This is, of course, utter nonsense, because if it were true then people who were good on the inside would never have to comb their hair or take a bath, and the whole world would smell even worse than it already does.

If an optimist had his left arm chewed off by an alligator, he might say, in a pleasant and hopeful voice, "Well, this isn't too bad. I don't have my left arm anymore, but at least nobody will ever ask me whether I am right-handed or left-handed," but most of us would say something more along the lines of "Aaaaah! My arm! My arm!"

One of the most difficult things

to think about in life is

one's regrets. Something will

happen to you, and you will do

the wrong thing, and for years

afterward you will wish you had

done something different.

If one's safety is threatened,
one often finds courage
one didn't know one had.

In times of extreme stress
one can often find energy
hidden in even the most
exhausted areas of the body.

In an emergency,

one often learns that one's

companions can be of even

less help in extraordinary

circumstances than they

are during an average evening.

Shyness is a curious thing,

because, like quicksand,

it can strike people at

any time, and also,

like quicksand,

it usually makes its

victims look down.

Frustration is an interesting emotional state, because it tends to bring out the worst in whoever is frustrated. Frustrated babies tend to throw food and make a mess. Frustrated citizens tend to execute kings and queens and make a democracy. And frustrated moths tend to bang up against lightbulbs and make light fixtures all dusty. But unlike babies, citizens, and moths, leeches are quite unpleasant to begin with.

The way sadness works is
one of the strangest
riddles of the world.

When someone is crying,

of course, the noble thing to do

is to comfort them.

But if someone is trying to hide

their tears, it may also be noble to

pretend you do not notice them,

so they will not be embarrassed.

Unless you have been very, very lucky, you have undoubtedly experienced events in your life that have made you cry. So unless you have been very, very lucky, you know that a good, long session of weeping can often make you feel better, even if your circumstances have not changed one bit.

9
AFFAIRS OF
THE HEART

Love can change a person
the way a parent can
change a baby—
awkwardly, and often
with a great deal of mess.

It is so rare in this world to
meet a trustworthy person
who truly wants to help you,
and finding such a person can
make you feel warm and safe,
even if you are in the middle
of a windy valley high up
in the mountains.

One of the remarkable things
about love is that,
despite very irritating people
writing poems and songs
about how pleasant it is,
it really is quite pleasant.

Bad circumstances

have a way of ruining things

that would otherwise

be pleasant.

It is often difficult to admit
that someone you love is
not perfect, or to consider
aspects of a person that are
less than admirable.

In love, as in life, one misheard word can be tremendously important. If you tell someone you love them, for instance, you must be absolutely certain that they have replied "I love you back" and not "I love your back" before you continue the conversation.

It is a curious thing, the death of a loved one. We all know that our time in this world is limited, and that eventually all of us will end up underneath some sheet, never to wake up. And yet it is always a surprise when it happens to someone we know. It is like walking up the stairs to your bedroom in the dark, and thinking there is one more stair than there is. Your foot falls down, through the air, and there is a sickly moment of dark surprise as you try and readjust the way you thought of things.

Grief, a type of sadness that

most often occurs when you

have lost someone you love,

is a sneaky thing, because it can

disappear for a long time,

and then pop back up

when you least expect it.

Everyone, at some point in their lives, wakes up in the middle of the night with the feeling that they are all alone in the world, and that nobody loves them now and that nobody will ever love them, and that they will never have a decent night's sleep again and will spend their lives wandering blearily around a love-less landscape, hoping desperately that their circumstances will improve, but suspecting, in their heart of hearts, that they will remain unloved forever. The best thing to do in these circumstances is to wake someone else up, so that they can feel this way, too.

10

A LIFE OF
MYSTERY

There are tiresome people who say that if you ever find yourself in a difficult situation, you should stop and figure out the right thing to do. But there are times in this harum-scarum world when figuring out the right thing to do is quite simple, but doing the right thing is simply impossible, and then you must do something else.

Saying that something
is half the battle is like
saying something is half
a sandwich, because it is
dangerous to announce
that something is half the
battle when the much more
difficult part might still be
waiting in the wings. . . .

As I'm sure you know,

the key to good eavesdropping

is not getting caught.

When listening at someone
else's door, always have an excuse
prepared so that when they
fling the door open to glare at you,
you will have something
reasonable to say.

In general, of course, a stranger who tries to get you into an automobile is anything but noble, and in general a person who quotes great American novelists is anything but treacherous, and in general a man who says you needn't worry about money, or a man who smokes cigarettes, is somewhere in between.

The trouble with doing something suspicious for a living is that your coworkers will likely be suspicious, too, and you will find yourself entangled in a web of suspicion, even during your lunch hour.

Having an aura of menace is like having a pet weasel, because you rarely meet someone who has one, and when you do it makes you want to hide under the coffee table.

There are many difficult

things in this world to hide,

but a secret

is not one of them.

It is very easy to say that the important thing is to try your best, but if you are in real trouble the most important thing is not trying your best, but getting to safety.

Normally it is not polite to go
into somebody's room
without knocking,
but you can make an
exception if the
person is dead,
or pretending to be dead.

Announcing your death
should be like announcing
that you are a lunar moth:
It must be done quietly
or it will not be believed.

II

THE MYSTERY OF LIFE

It is difficult, when faced
with a situation you cannot
control, to admit that
you can do nothing.

Morning is an important time of day, because how you spend your morning can often tell you what kind of day you are going to have. For instance, if you wake up to the sound of twittering birds, and find yourself in an enormous canopy bed, with a butler standing next to you holding a breakfast of freshly made muffins and hand-squeezed orange juice on a silver tray, you will know that your day will be a splendid one. If you wake up to the sound of church bells, and find yourself in a fairly big regular bed, with a butler standing next to you holding a breakfast of hot tea and toast on a plate, you will know that your day will be O.K. And if you wake up to the sound of somebody banging two metal pots together, and find yourself in a small bunk bed, with a nasty foreman standing in the doorway holding no breakfast at all, you will know that your day will be horrid.

Sometimes even in the most

unfortunate of lives there

will occur a moment or

two of good fortune.

Occasionally, events in one's life become clearer through the prism of experience, a phrase which simply means that things tend to become clearer as time goes on. For instance, when a person is just born, they usually have no idea what curtains are and spend a great deal of their first months wondering why on earth Mommy and Daddy have hung large pieces of cloth over each window in the nursery. But as the person grows older, the idea of curtains becomes clearer through the prism of experience. The person will learn the word "curtains" and notice that they are actually quite handy for keeping a room dark when it is time to sleep, and for decorating an otherwise boring window area. Eventually, they will entirely accept the idea of curtains, and may even purchase some curtains of their own, or venetian blinds, and it is all due to the prism of experience.

One wanders through life as
if wandering through a field in
the dark of night, wearing a
blindfold and very heavy shoes,
with a poisonous toad waiting
patiently beneath a clump of
weeds, knowing full well that
eventually you will step on him.

It is one of the peculiar truths of life that people often say things that they know full well are ridiculous. If someone asks you how you are, for example, you might automatically say "Fine, thank you," when in fact you have just failed an examination or been trampled by an ox. A friend might tell you, "I've looked everywhere in the world for my keys," when you know that they have actually only looked in a few places in the immediate area. Once I said to a woman I loved very much, "I'm sure that this trouble will end soon, and you and I will spend the rest of our lives together in happiness and bliss," when I actually suspected that things were about to get much worse.

Fate is like a strange,

unpopular restaurant,

filled with odd waiters who

bring you things you never

asked for and don't always like.

Deciding on the right thing to do in a situation is a bit like deciding on the right thing to wear to a party. It is easy to decide on what is wrong to wear to a party, such as deep-sea diving equipment or a pair of large pillows, but deciding what is right is much trickier. The truth is that you can never be sure if you have decided on the right thing until the party is over, and by then it is too late to go back and change your mind, which is why the world is filled with people doing terrible things and wearing ugly clothing.

It is very difficult to make

one's way in this world without

being wicked at one time or

another, when the world's way

is so wicked to begin with.

One of the greatest myths in the world—and the phrase "greatest myths" is just a fancy way of saying "big fat lies"—is that troublesome things get less and less troublesome if you do them more and more. People say this myth when they are teaching children to ride bicycles, for instance, as though falling off a bicycle and skinning your knee is less troublesome the fourteenth time you do it than it is the first time. The truth is that troublesome things tend to remain troublesome no matter how many times you do them, and that you should avoid doing them unless they are absolutely urgent.

One cannot spend
forever sitting and
solving the mysteries
of one's history.

12

AN OVERALL
FEELING OF DOOM
THAT ONE CANNOT
EVER ESCAPE
NO MATTER WHAT
ONE DOES

Destiny is something

you cannot escape,

such as death,

or a cheesecake that

has curdled,

both of which always

turn up sooner or later.

Everybody will die, of course, sooner or later. Circus performers will die, and clarinet experts will die, and you and I will die, and there might be a person who lives on your block, right now, who is not looking both ways before he crosses the street and who will die in just a few seconds, all because of a bus. Everybody will die, but very few people want to be reminded of that fact.

Assumptions are dangerous things to make, and like all dangerous things to make—bombs, for instance, or strawberry shortcake—if you make even the tiniest mistake you can find yourself in terrible trouble. For instance, one morning you might wake up and make the assumption that your bed was in the same place that it always was, even though you would have no real evidence that this was so. But when you got out of your bed, you might discover that it had floated out to sea, and now you would be in terrible trouble all because of the incorrect assumption that you'd made. You can see that it is better not to make too many assumptions, particularly in the morning.

Taking one's chances is like taking a bath, because sometimes you end up feeling comfortable and warm, and sometimes there is something terrible lurking around that you cannot see until it is too late and you can do nothing else but scream and cling to a plastic duck.

The thing you hope will never happen to you might just happen to someone else instead, who has been spending their life dreading the thing that will happen to you.

If you have ever found yourself sitting in darkness with a flashlight, you may have experienced the feeling that something is lurking just beyond the circle of light that a flashlight makes, and reading a poem about dead men is not a good way to make yourself feel better.

Many old folktales portray Death as a cloaked figure who knocks on the doors of the souls he has come to whisk away, but that is not always the way of the world. Sometimes Death may approach the door very slowly and very loudly, so that by the time he knocks everyone in the neighborhood is aware of his approach, or he may prefer to pick the lock of the back door and sit up all night in your kitchen until you stroll downstairs in your bathrobe and learn that he has been waiting for you, sitting in your favorite chair and rearranging your silverware when he got bored.

There are some who go through life with a shadow hanging over them, particularly if they live in a building which has long, wide awnings.

I heard once of a man who wanted desperately to be remembered after his death, so he spent his youth writing and rewriting his last words, and his old age repeating them every five minutes so that if he died at that moment the words he had prepared would be overheard by someone. At last, on his deathbed, someone asked him the time.

Waiting is

one of life's

hardships.

13

MISCELLANEOUS

Never look a

gift lion

in the mouth.

There are many, many things that are difficult in this life, but one thing that isn't difficult at all is figuring out whether someone is excited or not when they open a present. If someone is excited, they will often put exclamation points at the ends of their sentences to indicate their excited tone of voice. If they say "Oh!" for instance, the exclamation point would indicate that the person is saying "Oh!" in an excited way, rather than simply saying "Oh," with a comma after it, which would indicate that the present is somewhat disappointing.

Just about everything in this world is easier said than done, with the exception of "systematically assisting Sisyphus's stealthy, cyst-susceptible sister," which is easier done than said.

Of all the ridiculous expressions people use—and people use a great many ridiculous expressions—one of the most ridiculous is "No news is good news." "No news is good news" simply means that if you don't hear from someone, everything is probably fine, and you can see at once why this expression makes such little sense, because everything being fine is only one of many, many reasons why someone may not contact you. Perhaps they are tied up. Maybe they are surrounded by fierce weasels, or perhaps they are wedged tightly between two refrigerators and cannot get themselves out. The expression might well be changed to "No news is bad news," except that people may not be able to contact you because they have just been crowned king or are competing in a gymnastics tournament. The point is that there is no way to know why someone has not contacted you, until they contact you and explain themselves.

For this reason, the sensible expression would be "No news is no news," except that it is so obvious it is hardly an expression at all.

If you are allergic to a thing,

it is best not to put that thing in

your mouth, particularly

if the thing is cats.

Stealing, of course, is a crime, and a very impolite thing to do. But like most impolite things, it is excusable under certain circumstances. Stealing is not excusable if, for instance, you are in a museum and you decide that a certain painting would look better in your house, and you simply grab the painting and take it there. But if you were very, very hungry, and you had no way of obtaining money, it might be excusable to grab the painting, take it to your house, and eat it.

Sometimes, when someone tells

a ridiculous lie,

it is best to ignore it entirely.

The expression "following suit" is a curious one, because it has nothing to do with walking behind a matching set of clothing. If you follow suit, it means you do the same thing somebody else has just done. If all of your friends decided to jump off a bridge into the icy waters of an ocean or river, for instance, and you jumped in right after them, you would be following suit. You can see why following suit can be a dangerous thing to do, because you could end up drowning simply because somebody else thought of it first.

It is very unnerving to be

proven wrong, particularly

when you are really right and

the person who is really

wrong is the one who is

proving you wrong

and proving himself,

wrongly, right.

Right?

Having a personal philosophy
is like having a pet marmoset,
because it may be very
attractive when you acquire it,
but there may be situations
when it will not come in
handy at all.

The quoting of an aphorism, like the angry barking of a dog or the smell of overcooked broccoli, rarely indicates that something helpful is about to happen.